GREEN SMOOTHIES & PROTEIN DRINKS

JASON MANHEIM

PHOTOGRAPHY BY LEO QUIJANO II

Skyhorse Publishing

Skyhorse Publishing books may be purchased in bulk at special discounts for sales promotion, corporate gifts, fund-raising, or educational purposes. Special editions can also be created to specifications. For details, contact the Special Sales Department, Skyhorse Publishing, 307 West 36th Street, 11th Floor, New York, NY 10018 or info@skyhorsepublishing.com.

Skyhorse® and Skyhorse Publishing® are registered trademarks of Skyhorse Publishing, Inc. ®, a Delaware corporation.

www.skyhorsepublishing.com

10 9 8 7 6 5 4 3 2 1

Library of Congress Cataloging-in-Publication Data is available on file.
ISBN: 978-1-62087-601-5
Printed in China

Design by Adriann Helton

TABLE OF CONTENTS

Green Smoothie and Protein Drink Recipes

KEY

Post Work-out

Beauty

Kids/Beginner

Greens Lover

Savory

INTRODUCTION

In my first book, *The Healthy Green Drink Diet: Advice and Recipes to Energize, Alkalize, Lose Weight, and Feel Great*, I introduced the notion of supplementing your current diet with at least one green drink or smoothie a day. The idea is that not only will this give your body an extra boost of nutrients, but eventually you will naturally begin to crave these healthier foods. Without much conscious—and sometimes painfully annoying—effort, you can slowly replace unhealthy foods with healthier counterparts and your overall diet and well being will benefit because of it.

The previous book was very much a book for beginners. In it I went over the many varieties of greens, fruits, superfoods, and sweeteners as well as basic tips on growing, buying, saving, storing, and the equipment needed. In my new book I will pick up where we left off and dig deeper, while offering a quick recap of the essentials.

As in the previous book, there are 50 recipes all with matching photographs, ranging from novice to more advanced flavor profiles. However, this time around we will focus entirely on green smoothies (made using a blender) instead of a mix of both juicing and blending. In the chapter titled "More on Juicing vs. Blending," I will go over why I've eliminated juicing and why blending is where you should focus your efforts (unless digestion issues keep you from enjoying the benefits of fiber). This isn't to say juicing is *bad*, but that blending is juicing 2.0, if you will, and offers more bang for your buck.

We will also be focusing on how to turn your green smoothies in protein drinks. This is for those who want to use them for a post workout recovery or for more of a meal replacement rather than a starter. Most recipes will contain suggestions on the best types of protein to add.

WELLNESS:
Digestion, Detoxing, and Fighting Disease

Throughout this book I recommend, at the bare minimum, enjoying a green smoothie first thing in the morning to break your nightly fast. Not only is it a great way to consume a wide variety of nutrients in a quick, convenient package, but it also helps tremendously with digestion. This **should not** be an accompaniment to your normal breakfast, but rather a pre-breakfast. Wait at least an hour before eating any solid foods as this will minimize gas and bloating and maximize nutrient absorption from the green smoothie. This is not a hard and fast rule, but if you notice any excess gas and bloating, you may want to increase the time between your green smoothie and your regular meal.

The fiber is the magic here. This is why I strongly encourage you to think again before going the juicing route and instead opt for the colon cleansing, digestion powerhouse that whole green leaves and fruits provide. You can even add foods like flax seeds to bump that fiber content up more. And adding ginger to your green smoothies will further aid digestion by preventing gas when consuming common gas-producing foods like beans, fruit skins, and starchy vegetables.

Now let's focus on the method of "food combining," which in my opinion is simply a poor solution to an even greater underlying problem. *Food combining* is a term for the nutritional approach that encourages specific combinations of foods as central to good health and weight loss. Many believe that combining certain foods allows for the full digestion of nutrients and aids in the prevention of certain chronic metabolic diseases. Through observance, both personal and impersonal, I have come to realize that food combining is mostly a ridiculous notion.

While food combining does not help promote healthy digestion, combining unhealthy foods can actually have a negative effect. Our bodies are naturally equipped to digest the three constituents of food: protein, fat, and carbohydrates. Digestion begins the moment we smell or even think about food. This stimulates the secretion of digestive enzymes and we begin to salivate. Fat and carbs begin to digest as soon as they enter our mouths, so if we're not chewing properly to break down cellular walls, our digestion is hindered. Green smoothies are great because a high-powered blender has already done most of the initial break-down. However, it is important to drink your smoothies slowly and swish each sip around in your mouth a bit to combine it with the enzymes in your mouth. From there, we go to the stomach where acids begin to break down protein. If your stomach acid levels are low, then protein breakdown is hindered. Likewise, if you eat too much (especially processed foods high in trans fats) your gallbladder will struggle to produce bile needed to assist in fat digestion. In general, overeating causes our bodies to have a hard time keeping up with digestive enzyme secretion and the breaking down of fats, carbs, and protein is negatively affected. If our diets are high in cooked and processed foods, we are also denying ourselves essential enzymes from fresh, raw foods that are necessary for proper digestion.

Food combining problems are caused by a diet low in fresh, whole living foods that has ultimately altered the quantity, quality, and effectiveness of your digestive system and the enzymes it produces. This is why some people have issues when combining proteins and sugars. Most people adopting a more green-centric diet are coming from a place of unhealthiness so it will take some time for your body to heal itself. Once it does, you should see most of your food combining worries wash away.

First things first: We need to get to a place where our digestive system is functioning properly. Green smoothies are wonderful aids in this because they are so rich in vitamins, minerals, enzymes, and fiber; they make for a wonderful detox pillar. I do not advocate any form of juice-only detox (juice fasting, lemonade diet, etc.) as these usually contain high amounts of sugar and very little fiber. When detoxing, fiber is the number one aspect to consider. I recommend detoxing the way nature intended: whole foods with a foundation of fresh leafy greens and fruit.

Detox Tips:

- To detox using green smoothies, I recommend going no more than a week before slowly adding solid foods back into your diet.

- Stick with simple combinations throughout the day (using greens, fruits, and fats) and end your days with something savory, with little to no fruit.

- My favorite detox combinations are dandelion greens and lemon with perhaps an apple to sweeten it up a bit and maybe a slice of avocado.

- Remember to "chew" your smoothies (to get those digestive enzymes flowing) and play with quantities and different types of fats if bloating or gas is a major issue.

- Berries are a great, albeit expensive, way to add calories and limit excess sugar.

- Keep in mind that the first few days (and up to the entire week), depending on how unhealthy you are, you will feel sluggish and possibly worse than you did before starting the detox. This is because your body is eliminating waste that has built up over time.

Eventually, the easier it is for your body to eliminate waste (including toxins), the better your body will react to anything you throw at it, including the occasional slice of sugary cake.

While fruits contain a high amount of sugar (mostly fructose), the truth is most people actually lower their sugar intake after switching from sweets like soda, artificial sweeteners, sugary processed foods, etc. to a diet where the majority of sugar comes from fresh fruit. So, the fear of ingesting too much sugar is mostly a non-issue unless you have a condition where sugar intake should definitely be limited like diabetes, hypoglycemia, or candida. But again, the fiber comes to the rescue and slows down sugar absorption so that is definitely something to account for. Plus, if you're doing a detox, you need the extra calories and carbohydrates that the fruit provides.

Another benefit to consuming green smoothies regularly is how it affects your skin. After a few months, you'll notice cleaner, more vibrant skin, nails, and even hair. The added vitamins and minerals are at play here. Try adding foods like pumpkin, coconut, sweet potato, protein (pasteurized eggs), and avocado to increase the effects.

I'm not going to go into specific remedies for certain diseases for a few reasons: One, I am not a doctor. Two, natural remedies that work for one person don't always work for another. Three, certain medications interfere with things like grapefruit juice so ultimately you want to consult your doctor for specific recommendations.

That said, there isn't a disease I can think of that green smoothies can't help tackle in some way or another.

- Green smoothies are packed with flavonoids and antioxidants (great cancer fighters), vitamins, minerals, enzymes, carbs, fats, and protein.

- Need to watch your sugar intake because of diabetes, hypoglycemia, or candida? No problem—the fiber in green smoothies slows the absorption of sugars. Or, simply eliminate the fruit and go savory.

- Skin problems? You can take it even further and mash fresh aloe, cucumber, avocado, and even plantains to make a great cleansing face mask.

- Problems with IBS (irritable bowel syndrome)? Avoid fruit-heavy green smoothies (go savory) and greens like broccoli, cabbage, dandelion greens, and beet greens. Also, limit your smoothie intake to no more than 16 ounces at a time; portion size is important when dealing with IBS. Simple green smoothies work the best: banana, blueberries, spinach, and water. Another great recipe for those suffering from IBS: frozen pineapple, celery, ginger, banana, and water. Consider supplementing with probiotics or digestive enzymes before a meal heavy in fats.

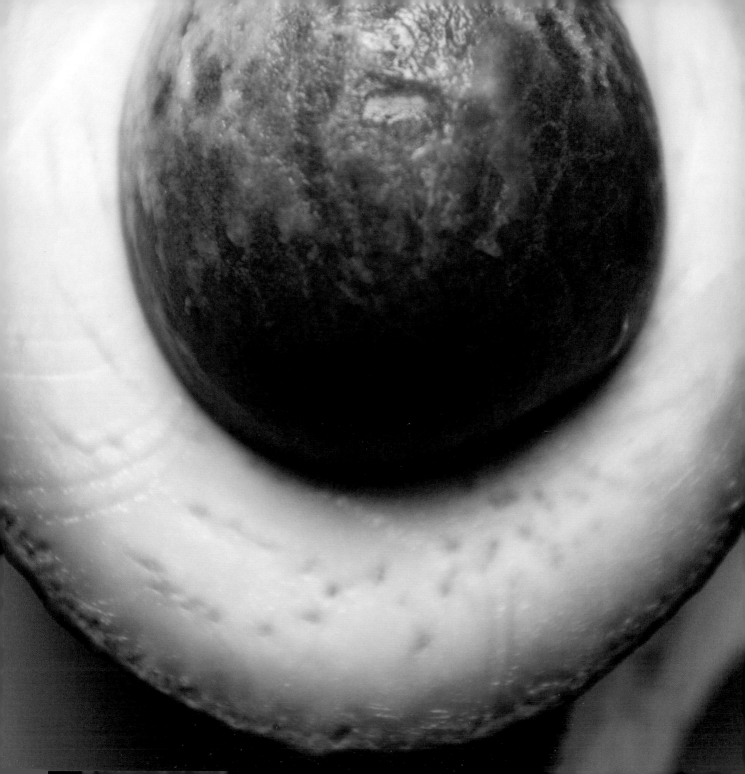

BODY:
Fitness, Diet, and Weight Loss

These days, the general population is quickly finding out that the diet we have struggled with for so many years, the diet that was supposed to keep us healthy and maintain a reasonable weight, is a load of BS. You know the diet I'm speaking of: low fat, high carb.

First, let's take a look at the different types of fat:

- **Trans fatty acids** (hydrogenated)—Created when processed vegetable oils are (partially) hydrogenated to make the oil less likely to spoil. It actually makes the fat harder at room temperature (as opposed to its natural liquid form), which is great for processed food manufacturers but not at all for our arteries. This process destroys essential fatty acids. Many foods that are labeled as "low fat" (to conform to the "low fat, high carb" diet I spoke of above) contain a surprising amount of hydrogenated oils and extra sugar. Avoid this fat at all costs.

- **Saturated**—The big bad, right? That's what we've been taught for most of our lives. The truth is excess saturated fats (and most fats in excess for that matter) should be avoided by people who are already overweight and maintain a diet high in processed food and added sugars. This is common sense. However, the kicker is that fats actually help slow the absorption of sugar, which is a good thing. For healthy, active people, saturated fat is quite healthy. Somewhat contrary to what food manufacturers and their ilk would have us believe, diets high in saturated fat have been known to aid weight loss, but only in people who remove processed foods and added sugars (starches) from the rest of their diet. Saturated fats come primarily from meat (and coconuts) and humans have been eating animal fat for millions of years. In fact, our bodies actually prefer to use it as an energy source instead of ingested sugars, given that our diets contain mostly whole, fresh foods. It seems strange, to say the least, that our bodies' natural functions would prefer something that harms us. Much research has been done in small scales to suggest saturated fats are not the evil, fat-inducing, heart-attack bad guy of the food world, but more research is sorely needed in this area. Given that most of the world (especially the United States) is governed by another type of green (money)—and that large corporations in control of our food supplies, advertising, and prescription medication have a vested interest in telling us what is "healthy" or not—convincing people to take another look at saturated fat is a difficult feat. Perhaps we should push our cattle farmers to start a "saturated is healthy" campaign . . .

- **Polyunsaturated** (PUFA)—This one is a mixed bag. It is wonderful if we're talking about Omega-3 and Omega-6 fatty acids (along with other essential fatty acids) but these fats can oxidize remarkably fast by heating and exposure to air, light, and moisture. Many people take Omega-3 supplements because they think they're deficient in the essential fatty acids, but if you incorporate green smoothies into your diet along with a whole foods diet (foods that are unprocessed and unrefined), you should be just fine (despite the exposure to air, light, etc. via whipping in a blender if you drink it right away). Not to mention, most people don't purchase Omega-3 oil from sources that have handled and stored it correctly, so you end up getting something that does far more damage than it otherwise would prevent. However, vegans and vegetarians may consider taking fish oil supplements with a 1:1 ratio of Omega-3 to Omega-6 with EPA and DHA. Natural sources of polyunsaturated fatty acids can be found in nuts, fish, kiwi, chia seeds, flax, and leafy greens.

Green Smoothies and Protein Drinks

- **Monounsaturated**—Of all the different types of fat, polyunsaturated is considered the "healthy fat." Olive oil is the best source. It's high in polyphenols, antioxidants, and oleic acid, which is a great alternative to animal-based saturated fats for vegans and vegetarians if you roll that way.

Now, let us break down different types of carbohydrates:

- **Simple**—Sometimes referred to as simple sugars, this carbohydrate is in its simplest form and is more easily digested than complex carbs. These are foods like refined sugars, candy, cookies, and fruit. They have names like fructose (from fruit), sucrose, glucose, dextrose, maltose, and lactose. Some, of course, are better than others (which also depends on what is accompanying them).

- **Complex**—Also called starches. These need to be broken down into their simple form before they can be used. These are foods like grains, vegetables, nuts, seeds, rice, and again, fruit.

Subcategory of carbs:

- **Fiber**—Technically a complex carbohydrate, there are two types of fiber: soluble and insoluble. Soluble fiber dissolves in water and turns into a gel-like substance, which slows down digestion. It fills your stomach and makes you feel full thereby controlling weight and slowing the absorption of sugars, which is yet another reason for diabetics to embrace the green smoothie. Sources of soluble fiber include apples, pears, mango, banana, papaya, kiwi, avocado, and strawberries. Insoluble fiber increases the movement of food and the cleaning and removing of intestinal toxins through your digestive tract. It is the broom of your digestive system. Sources include: greens and other veggies, fruit skins and peels, nuts, seeds, and grains.

- **High Glycemic**—These are carbs that raise your blood sugar level very quickly and cause high amounts of insulin to be released to return your blood sugar back to normal. How? It converts the glucose in your body to fat. Sources include potatoes, white breads, corn, carrots, etc.

- **Low Glycemic**—These foods cause a low rise in blood sugar levels. Sources include most fruits and vegetables, legumes, nuts, etc.

- **Refined (processed)**—These carbs have been altered to increase shelf life and are what you want to avoid at all costs. Sources include white breads, pasta, cookies, etc.

When eating carbohydrates, your body first breaks them down into simple sugars that are then absorbed into the bloodstream. As more sugar is absorbed, the pancreas releases insulin, which helps move sugar out of the bloodstream and into cells where it's primarily used as a source of energy. Naturally, complex carbs break down slower than simple carbs, which give you that full feeling and provide energy over a longer period of time. Because simple sugars are absorbed much faster, your body quickly fills to "energy capacity" and the excess sugar is converted to fatty acids, which eventually leads to unhealthy weight gain.

So, the takeaway here is that the "low fat, high carb" diet does indeed work, but only if you are currently overweight and only if the types of fat and carbs consumed are explicitly stated. For instance, a fruit and vegetable-centric diet with low amounts of poly and monounsaturated fats, with your carbs coming from the fruits in your green smoothies and not from processed foods and grains, is ideal for fat-loss. However, for

the average person, equal attention to healthy fats (even high-fat diets), carbs from whole foods, and protein is ideal. Fat is not the enemy, bad sugars are. (Think of fat as lubrication in the same way a car needs clean oil to function in tip-top shape.) Replace your grain carbs with fruit carbs and watch the fat drop.

It's important to note that portion size can completely ruin your weight-loss progress, no matter how healthy the foods are that you eat. Replacing two large pizzas with two gallons of green smoothies every meal is certainly a better call, but losing the poundage may prove difficult.

Common Weight-Loss Myths:

1. All fats are created equal. We know better now, right? Fats are essential, but it's important to focus on healthy fats when beginning a weight-loss regimen like olive oil, avocado, and fish oil. After removing all refined carbs, feel free to add saturated fats like meat and coconut to your diet, as well.

2. Reducing calories is all that matters. True to a point, but it's more important to know where the calories are coming from. Choose fresh, whole, living foods and supplement with a green smoothie here and there. Once that is cemented, work on lowering your portions and you're golden.

3. Carbs make you fat. We know now that there are good carbs and bad carbs. Fresh fruit is the best source of carbs for anyone, let alone folks looking to lose weight. Plus, fruit is high in fiber and regulates your blood sugar. Avoid the refined carbs at all costs.

4. Skip meals. Fasting is a lousy way to lose weight. You're essentially starving yourself and in most cases your body will go into this "starvation mode" and store calories as fat because it is tricked into believing that you don't have access to food. Pro tip: NEVER skip breakfast. It gets your metabolism moving and supplies you with much needed energy and nutrition.

5. Skip the snacks between meals. Snacking is a great way to feel satiated between meals and it will allow you to eat less during main meals. Guess what? Green smoothies make for great snacks between meals.

6. Avoid weight lifting and strength training unless you want to bulk up. This is a concern for most women. Truth is, it takes tremendous effort and very heavy weights to bulk up. Aside from green smoothies, there is nothing better you can do for your body than adding a strength training routine. This is especially important for those who are very overweight and/or live a mostly sedentary lifestyle, as your muscles may have atrophied under all that fat.

Using green smoothies as a meal replacement is something I would consider a detox and not a weight-loss plan. A diet focused on losing weight should be a slight variation to the diet you will enjoy once you hit your ideal weight. It shouldn't be completely different, as that makes it difficult to follow, maintain, and find enjoyment throughout the process.

That being said, there is nothing wrong with detoxing for a week before starting a new weight-loss diet. If you're insistent on replacing a meal with a green smoothie, I would suggest breakfast. Make sure to include fruit, greens, and fat all while keeping the following in mind:

Tips for Weight-Loss Green Smoothies:

1. **Limit fats**. Adding too much fat along with fruits may cause gas and bloating for some people and could also interfere with how your body uses the sugar in the fruit, which could lead to weight gain. Introduce more fat periodically to test how it affects you.

2. **Limit fruits**. This one is only relevant if you continue to eat processed sugary foods. If you have successfully eliminated those foods from your diet, feel free to eat fruit regularly.

3. **Avoid canned fruit**. Almost all canned fruit contains added sugar and preservatives. Fresh fruit (organic if possible) contain more nutrients. Go frozen if fresh is unavailable.

4. **Avoid sweeteners**. Fruit should be your only source of sweet. Try a ripe banana or mango before grabbing the honey, agave, or anything else.

5. **Avoid dairy**. Usually contains excess sugar that you don't need. Your calcium and vitamins will come from the fruit and greens.

6. **Avoid store-bought fruit juice and nut milks**. Again, these often contain sugars and preservatives that hinder weight loss. Try soaking some almonds in water overnight and make your own almond milk.

7. **Use dark leafy greens that are protein-rich**. These are your main source of vitamins, minerals, and enzymes. Add as much as you want.

8. **Maintain a ratio of 1–2 cups of fruit to 2–4 cups of greens and 1–2 cups of water**.

9. **Consider adding extra fiber**. When losing weight and ridding ourselves of toxins, fiber is key. Try adding chia seeds, apples with the skin on, blueberries, etc.

Your Weight-Loss Game Plan:

- Consider starting with a green smoothie detox for about a week or so.

- Never skip breakfast and always either have a green smoothie an hour or so before your normal breakfast or replace your breakfast entirely with a green smoothie.

- Replace snacks with 16 ounces of green smoothie. Pro tip: Make a big batch for breakfast and drink it throughout the day.

- Adjust your regular diet. Remove processed foods and added sugars and eat more whole foods.

- Get some daily exercise (about 30 minutes) and at least one day a week, take on a more strenuous strength routine.

- Eliminate the dieting pills, pre-packaged shakes, or any other "miracle cure." These will never be a part of your regular diet once you lose the weight, so why on earth use them now?

- Find a friend to join you. Motivation wanes sometimes and it's always nice to have backup.

Now let's take a look at the other side of the spectrum: weight *gain*. There are two types of people to consider here, the first is someone who is naturally thin and may be a vegetarian or vegan and is most likely finding it a challenge to gain weight on a plant-based diet. The other type is an athletic person trying to incorporate green smoothies into their regimen.

The former is most likely not gaining weight because they are not consuming enough calories. Simple as that. A quick and easy method would be to increase the amount of healthy fats like coconut and avocado—which luckily for us is easy to do with green smoothies. However, we want to maintain overall health, so while increasing fat content is a start, we should also choose other calorie dense foods like sweet potato, mango, banana, dates, and figs. From there, try increasing your serving sizes by an ounce or two per week and make sure to stay active—30 minutes of moderate activity per day and 1-2 days per week of heavy movement/lifting for 20 minutes or so—we want that weight to come from muscle, not fat. You can even try adding 30 grams of protein to your morning green smoothie (with 30 minutes of waking) to increase fat burning so we can more easily put those calories and nutrients towards building a healthy weight. You can learn more about this idea from *The 4-Hour Body* by Timothy Ferriss.

The latter type of person is much easier to deal with. Most athletes already drink a post-workout protein shake so simply toss that concoction into a blender, add a handful of fresh greens, and you have yourself a green protein smoothie with added vitamins and minerals. There are a quite few recipes in this book that are great for adding protein supplements to and I have marked them accordingly.

Protein options:
- Nut butters (almond, macadamia, Brazil)
- Protein powders (whey, hemp, egg)
- Chia seeds (or flax seeds)
- Whole, raw milk (and yogurt)

So there we are; green smoothies can be an incredibly powerful tool in helping turn your health around. While green smoothies offer tremendous benefit on their own, your best bet is to use them to help transition the rest of your diet into a more healthy one. And never forget to be active. A sedentary lifestyle helps no one, even those that maintain incredibly healthy diets.

VARIETY:
A Diverse Diet Is Important

I'm lazy. Especially when it comes to things I find myself regularly repeating. These days I spend my time coding websites for small businesses, so I'm familiar with (and get a lot of enjoyment out of) optimizing chunks of code so as not to repeat myself several times. I approach my life in a similar manner and so naturally I want to automate as many bodily necessities as possible. This includes eating, or rather, my diet.

Early on in my green smoothie research and test phases, I realized (and you'll soon discover why this is completely wrong) that all I needed to do was come up with one combination of fruits, greens, superfoods, and fats that tasted relatively well together and was easy to buy in bulk. My ambrosia so to speak that could be consumed multiple times per day, with minimal prep effort and maximum nutrition. I was so excited. The smoothie was some variation of spinach, pumpkin purée, blueberries, coconut (milk, oil, and water), banana, and orange. The flavor wasn't terrible, and all of these ingredients could be purchased at my local Trader Joe's. Now I could focus on optimizing other parts of my life as it seemed as if I broke the diet code, right? Wrong.

About a month or two into my new green smoothie regimen, I read an article about the oxalic acid levels in spinach and how repetitive ingestion can lead to calcium oxalate kidney stones. This, naturally, scared the heck out of me. I can't imagine many things more frightening than having to pass a rock through my urethra. No thanks. My fear sparked further study and I soon discovered that oxalic acid in spinach isn't the only harmful reason to avoid eating the same type of green over and over. In comes alkaloids.

Alkaloids are a group of naturally occurring chemical compounds that are produced by many different organisms, including green leafy vegetables. You've no doubt heard of some of these alkaloids. Morphine is one that comes from the dried sap (called opium) of the poppy. Another helps you clear the fog after a late night and early morning and is often enjoyed warm with a splash of cream—you guessed it, caffeine. There are plenty more, but we'll focus on the different alkaloids specific to green leafy vegetables.

Alkaloids are toxic in large quantities, but in small amounts they are quite harmless and even strengthen the immune system by allowing the body's natural healing system to build up a sort of immunity. Remember the iocane powder scene in *The Princess Bride*? This idea is also the basis for homeopathic remedies.

Consuming the same type of leafy green for extended periods of time (weeks to months) without changing it up will allow the same type of alkaloid to build up in your system. This poisoning can cause all sorts of symptoms from loss of appetite, to tingling sensations, to low energy and sluggishness. This is the exact opposite of what we are trying to achieve. So how do we stop this? Simple, rotate your favorite greens, as alkaloids differ from green to green and variety will keep any one from building up to toxic levels. As a bonus, variation will allow for a wider range of vitamins, minerals, and enzymes in your diet. I recommend swapping out greens either every 1–3 days or just add a variety to each smoothie.

In the end, my diet optimization had to be knocked back a level, but the variety I enjoy now is well worth it. For your convenience, I have included on the following page a list of edible greens for your rotation pleasure.

- alfalfa sprouts
- amaranth
- arugula
- basil
- beet greens
- bok choy
- broccoli
- brussels sprouts
- burdock
- cabbages
- cactus leaves
- carrot tops
- celery
- chard
- chickweed
- cilantro
- clover
- collards
- dandelion greens
- dill
- endive
- escarole
- fennel
- fenugreek sprouts
- frisee
- garlic grass
- grape leaves
- kale
- lamb's quarters
- mache
- mint
- mizuna
- mustard greens
- oregano
- radicchio
- red clover
- romaine
- parsley
- plantain
- purslane
- sorrel
- spinach
- sunflower sprouts
- tarragon
- turnip greens
- watercress
- wheatgrass

Note: Sprouts contain higher amounts of alkaloids (as a defense mechanism to protect from animals eating the young plants) so it's important to limit them a bit more than you would other greens. They also contain more nutrients than they do when fully developed.

Please be mindful when choosing wild edibles, as some toxic and even deadly plants have a similar appearance to their healthy counterparts. If you're unsure, skip it and go for something you're familiar with.

More on Juicing Vs. Blending

Here we'll discuss some of the most popular "benefits" to juicing and blending, and I will attempt to convince you that blending is almost always preferable. If, however, you are a diehard juicing fan and it's helped you become healthier or fight off disease, please, by all means, listen to your body and continue to juice. I only ask that you hear the counter arguments and perhaps switch to blending for a trial month to compare.

First up is oxidation. Oxidation is basically the process by which food is exposed to oxygen and begins to decompose. Cut an apple in half and leave it on your countertop for five minutes. Notice the browning? That means the apple is beginning to oxidize, and the longer it sits exposed, the fewer vitamins and minerals are available for you to consume. Many people believe juicing is better than blending because blending whips air into your drink thereby causing faster oxidation. This is true to a certain degree. However, blending does not eliminate any of the fibrous material (like juicing does) which can, in fact, decrease the rate at which your drink oxidizes. The reason for this is blending breaks open more cell walls than juicing does, which allows more antioxidants to release into smoothies.

You can test this by doing a simple experiment. Take a handful of grapes and one apple and toss them in a blender. Do the same with a juicer. Put both into separate glasses, set them side-by-side, and see which one turns color (brownish) faster. I'll save you some time: it's the juice. So what does this tell us? Well, if for whatever reason we absolutely need to pull the most vitamins and minerals out of our fruits and vegetables in a concentrated fashion, and we're consuming it right away (storing juice is almost impossible while smoothies last up to three days properly stored), then juicing may be your best bet. But then we miss out on storability, fiber, and satiation. And some studies have found, with specific fruits and greens, that smoothies have less oxidation even when consuming right away.

Next up is the idea that juicing gives you a quick nutritional boost. This is also true, but let us dig a bit deeper. Juicing gives a quick nutritional boost because there is essentially no fibrous material to digest and the vitamins, minerals, and enzymes enter your bloodstream almost immediately after consumption. But how necessary is this? Why would we ever really need to pump so much nutrition into our bloodstream so quickly? The answer is, we don't. Unless, of course, fiber digestion is particularly hard on your body due to some disease and juicing is the only effective way to increase nutrients.

Then we have the energy boost argument. This comes primarily from the fact that juicing eliminates fiber, causing faster absorption of sugars. It's essentially a sugar rush you're feeling. Naturally, this is bad for diabetics or folks dealing with candida. Smoothies, though, don't suffer this fate. The fiber from the greens slow down the absorption of sugar from the fruit.

And then there is waste and cost effectiveness. Juicing requires more than twice the amount of fruits and veggies, and when you're through, there is quite a bit of dry, tasteless fiber left. This can be added as a thickener to soups and other recipes or added to your compost heap if you have one. Expect to drop two to three times the amount of money to maintain a juicing regime.

Many prominent juicing proponents suggest that blending is inferior to juicing because blending bypasses the chewing process, which is essential for proper digestion. First of all, you should be swishing the liquid (juice or smoothie) around in your mouth before each swallow to activate digestive enzymes in the mouth. Second, this is a supplement; it should not eliminate greens from the rest of your diet or any other food for that matter. And third, yes, blending does bypass the chewing process, but so does juicing.

And finally, there is what folks refer to as "food combining." The idea is that when combining fruits and vegetables, enzyme inhibitors butt up against digestive enzymes and may cause irritation in the intestines and poor nutrient absorption. More specifically, this is purported to be caused by starchy foods like carrots, broccoli, cabbage, and others. If anything, this is an argument against juicing since there is a greater variance of ingredients available, while blending is just concerned with fruits and greens (as opposed to the broad "vegetables"). Personally, I have noticed many times that combining sweet fruits with starchy vegetables cause excess gas, so that's what I try to avoid. In short, there is no credible and intensive scientific evidence to suggest that combining certain foods is "bad" for us. Logically, it just seems like a ridiculous notion, doesn't it? Everyone is different and reacts to food likewise. It's important to listen to our bodies to see how we're affected by certain foods and combinations and then act accordingly.

Bottom line: If you're dealing with digestion issues where minimizing mass in your stomach is essential, light juicing may be the way to go. Otherwise, blending offers so much more for a better price.

LOCAL:
Farmer's Markets, and Sustainability

For the sake of economic self-interest, we have begun to destroy our precious farmland and the ecological integrity of our entire planet. Eating local is a solution that I believe solves a problem that American society has been battling for many years. By eating local, we eliminate the need to spend countless dollars transporting food across seas and borders, mass advertising, packaging, refrigeration for extended periods of time. It allows for improved food quality given that the food is in our own backyard, so to speak. It contributes to the local economy and saves precious farmland that is constantly being destroyed to develop residential and commercial property since we're relying on large corporate farms that mass produce using pointless government subsidies. Instead, communities could be built around local farms to create foods that actually meet the needs of the people it is serving. It's about creating a society and food system that will last and is interested in utilizing natural resources that the area provides. It allows for people to reconnect with what it means to share a meal and allows for a real, meaningful understanding of where our food comes from, who produces it, and the consequences of allowing big business to control our health.

The first step to getting involved is to go out at least once a week to a local Farmer's Market and meet the people who are passionate about creating local, sustainable food systems and, while you're there, stock up on organic greens and fruits for your green smoothies. Try eating only the foods that are in season in your particular area.

Not only will you be voting with your wallet, but cycling fruits and veggies by season is a great, all natural way to vary your nutrient sources. It's a win for your body, your peers, and the planet as a whole.

KIDS:
Green Smoothies for the Little Ones

As adults, many of the foods and flavors we enjoy the most were cultivated during our younger years. My love for Mexican food, no doubt, comes from the numerous tacos and burritos my family would indulge in on a weekly basis—whether homemade or from our favorite local spot. If you were to cut me, I'm certain I would bleed salsa.

My mother was also quite the health nut during my childhood years, so vegetables, including a wide variety of greens, made an appearance at every meal. I never needed the typical "eat your veggies and you can have dessert" push because I was introduced to those flavors early on, was given them regularly, and ultimately developed a taste for them that is mirrored in my diet today.

This, I believe, is why consistently introducing your children to healthy foods as early as possible—even in the womb—will do wonders not only for their current well being but also for the way they approach their diet far into the future when you no longer have control over what they do and do not eat.

I'm sure this comes as no surprise, but green smoothies are a wonderful way to introduce your children to healthier foods. It isn't always a walk in the park, though, so let's go over some ways to make this process easier—especially for picky eaters.

- To start, you'll probably want to use more fruits than greens since sweet flavors are universally delicious.

- Stick to ingredients that are light and familiar like spinach, banana, orange, strawberry, or even chocolate.

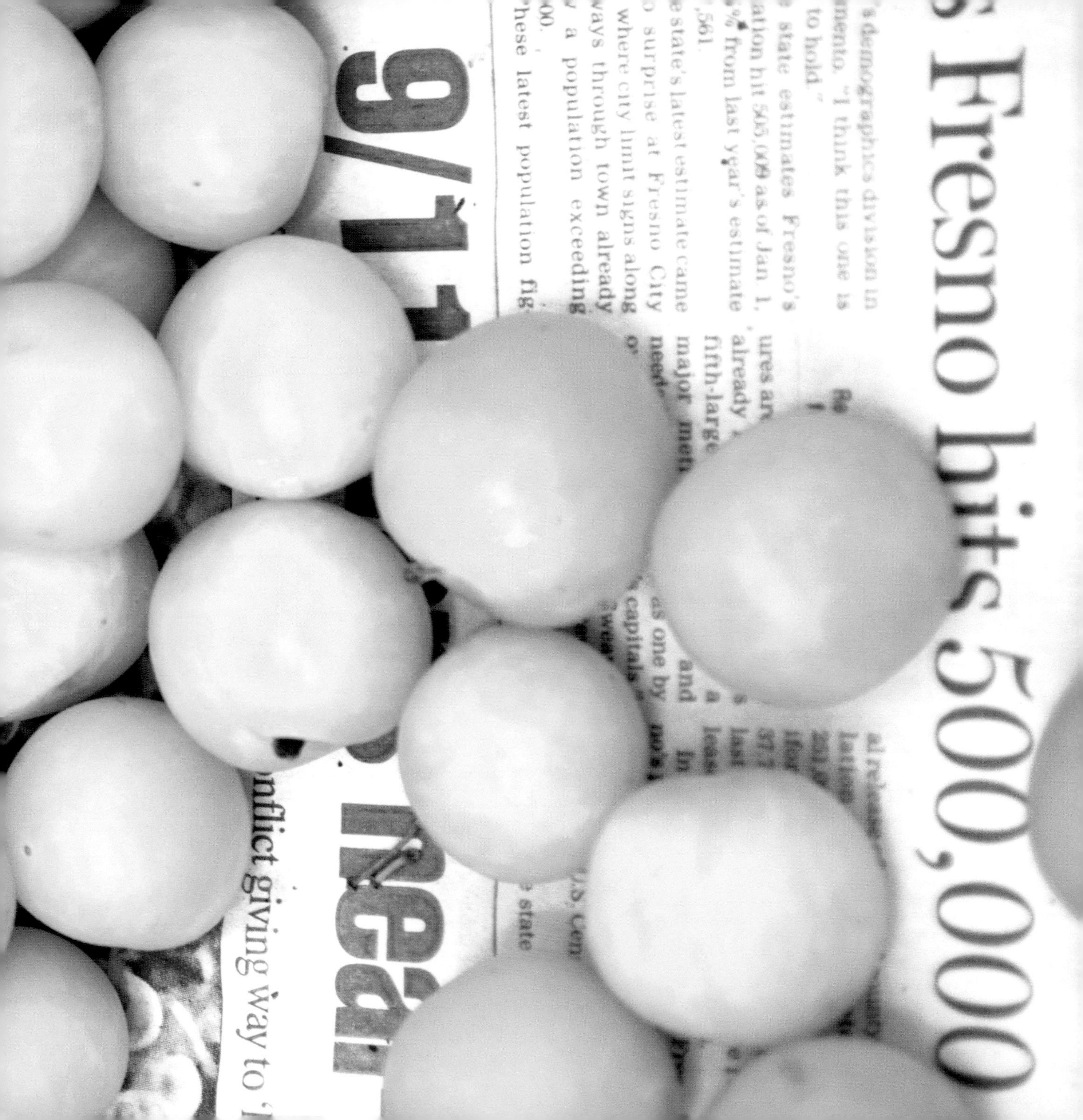
Fresno hits 500,000

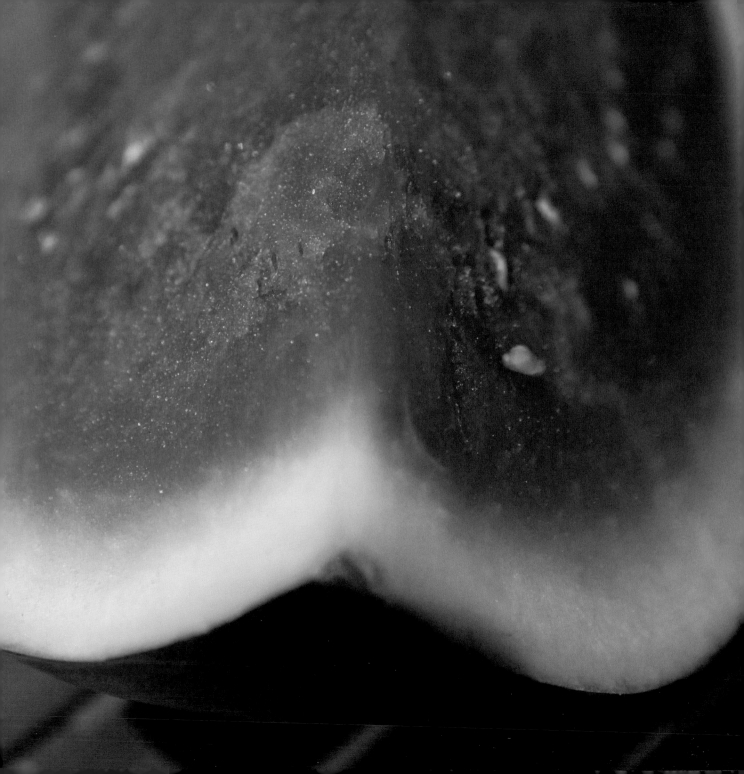

- It's important to be a role model, so it's good to have your children see you making and drinking green smoothies.

- Educate. Teach your children everything you learn about nutrition. Telling them the "why" regarding dietary choices is infinitely more impactful than simply telling them what to eat without explanation.

- Try adding small amounts of greens to smoothies they already enjoy and slowly add more over time.

- Add delicious toppers like sliced strawberries, dark chocolate shavings, a cherry, etc.

- Put one of those twirly straws in it.

- Set up a bunch of tiny cups and have a competition to see who can drink the most shots (always let them win)—this also prepares them for college.

- Tell them it's strength or beauty ooze (if it's green in color).

- Put the smoothie in an opaque cup so they don't see the strange color.

- Have your kids go grocery shopping with you and let them help pick out greens and fruits for your smoothies.

- Prep and experiment together. Try adding different variations and continuously taste test to see what they like better.

There are some recipes in this book that are geared towards beginners and kids, as they have a higher ratio of fruits to greens, but keep in mind that the ultimate goal is to eliminate as many fruits (sugar) as possible. Kids acclimate to these new flavors faster than adults so when they do, opt for the recipes with higher greens.

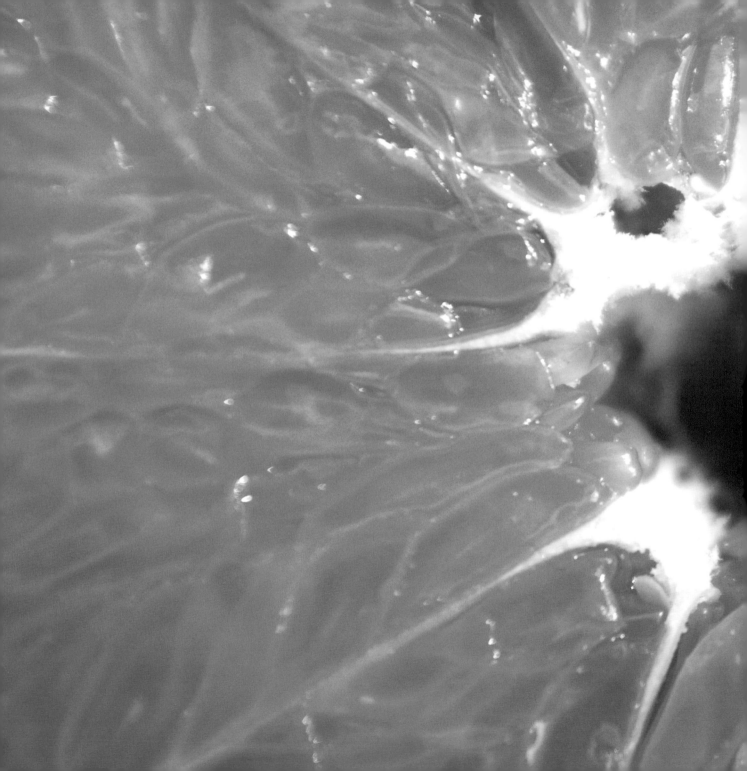

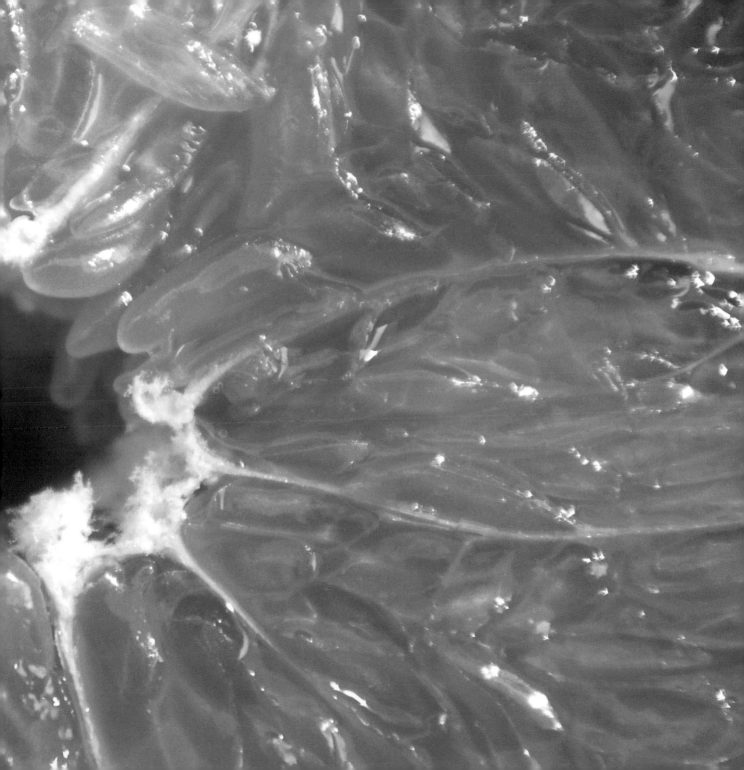

Green Smoothie Q & A

The following list of questions comes directly from you, dear readers. I have answered your questions from the first book, *The Healthy Green Drink Diet: Advice and Recipes to Energize, Alkalize, Lose Weight, and Feel Great*, that you emailed, posted to Facebook, Tweeted, and submitted through HealthyGreenDrink.com.

How much should I drink per day?

If your green smoothies consist primarily of greens and very little fruit, the sky's the limit as they say. At the very least you should shoot for 2–4 cups. Sometimes, I'll drink as much as half a gallon in one day.

If your goal is weight-loss, I suggest an 8-oz. glass of green smoothies before every meal. This will give you the nutrients you need and suppress your appetite enough so you're not gorging on other less nutritious foods.

Can I eat too many greens?

No. Since blending breaks down the fruits and greens better than you can naturally through just eating a salad normally, you can consume more nutrients by drinking green smoothies. This, of course, requires fewer greens than you otherwise would eat daily. A good rule of thumb is to eat at least two large bunches of greens per day or blend about half that amount. You want more? Go for it. Just make sure you're rotating the types of greens you're eating.

How much is a "bunch" of greens?

A bunch of greens is usually the amount in a small head of lettuce. Or, the amount you can comfortably hold in one hand. This usually amounts to about three packed cups.

How long do green smoothies keep?

Green smoothies keep up to three days in a cooler or refrigerator. However, it is best to consume as soon as possible. The longer you let the smoothie sit, the more nutrients oxidize and become less potent.

Can I freeze my smoothies and/or greens?

If you have excess greens and can't consume them before they go bad, by all means, freeze them. This works well for folks who bring in large harvests or can only make it to a market once every week or two. This will lower nutrient potency but not nearly as much as cooking greens or using slightly rotted greens. I have never needed to freeze an entire smoothie (just don't make as much if you can't drink it all . . . or keep it in the refrigerator for up to three days) but often times when I make a large batch, I'll pour off a cup or two into a few ice cube trays and use them instead of ice for future green smoothies. Again, this lessens the potency of the nutrients, but not by much.

Are green powders better, the same, or worse?

Fresh, living, vibrant greens are naturally better than powders. The process of tossing a bunch of fresh greens and some fruit into a blender couldn't be any easier, so there should be no need to resort to powders. However, the green powders aren't without their uses. When traveling or anywhere blending is impractical, mixing a scoop or two with fresh water will get the job done.

Some people like to add green powder in addition to fresh greens in their smoothies. This is a huge waste of money. If you have the option, go fresh every time.

I'm concerned about oxalic acid in spinach. Should I be?

Oxalic acid can bind with minerals (most notably, calcium) and make them inaccessible to the body. Eating foods high in oxalic acid (like spinach) on a regular basis over a period of months may leach these minerals and can even cause kidney stones. Calcium oxalate stones are the most common type of kidney stone and are formed when calcium crystallizes with oxalates. Most health professionals will suggest limiting foods with high oxalic acid levels in people who have previously had a kidney stone, but is an area of controversy in clinical nutrition as far as restriction.

Spinach has a bad rap for some reason, but many other foods have high level of oxalic acid as well, like nuts, seeds, grains, soy, berries, and more. The key is to vary your intake of foods—variety wins.

I'm concerned about too many alkaloids from the greens. Should I be?

Not unless you're eating the same type of greens every day for an extended period of time (months). Alkaloids are dangerous in large quantities and the same type can build up in your body if you don't vary your greens consumption. I suggest you read the chapter on "variety" to learn more.

I'm concerned about the amount of fruit/sugar I use. How much is too much?

If you suffer from diabetes, hypoglycemia, or candida, you certainly want to watch your sugar intake. Likewise, if you're trying to lose weight. The "green" taste can be hard to get used to, so many people try to mask it with sweet fruits. Instead, try using fruits with a low-glycemic index like berries, use greens that are less potent in flavor, or go for a savory green smoothie instead since they rarely contain fruit.

I hear grapefruit interferes with prescription medications. Is that true?

Grapefruit has been known to affect how the body metabolizes certain medications thereby leading to either less absorption or increased levels of the medication in your bloodstream—both of which can be dangerous.

These interactions can happen up to three days after ingesting grapefruit so separating consumption between meals or breakfast and dinner is useless. Certain medications for treating high blood pressure, high cholesterol, heart arrhythmia, depression, HIV, and more have been linked to this effect so if you are indeed taking any prescription medications, talk to your doctor first and he or she can confirm conflicts or offer alternatives.

I'm a vegetarian/vegan, what about protein?

Unless you are doing some heavy weight training or are involved in strenuous athletic activities, you should be getting all the protein you need from your regular diet and green smoothie supplements. Maintain a wide variety of fruits and vegetables and you'll be sure to get your fill of essential amino acids. Contrary to what most people think, greens provide a surprising amount of protein. If you do need extra protein, try adding protein powders to your smoothies.

When I'm lifting, I just add greens to my regular post-workout protein drink for an added boost of nutrition.

I'm vegan and green smoothies don't contain any Vitamin B12. Should I take supplements?

Most people get their Vitamin B12 from meats and dairy products, as plants contain very little if any. But being vegan, I'm sure you're already aware of this. I will refrain

from trying to convince you that maintaining a vegan diet isn't as healthy as some would have you believe. Instead, I suggest you have some bloodwork done and find out if you are indeed deficient in Vitamin B12. If so, there are plenty of B12 supplements available, and you shouldn't hesitate to take them or any other vitamin you may be deficient in.

I experimented with veganism for almost a year, and despite the lack of meat and dairy, I was never deficient in B12. Likewise, many raw vegans I know (who also drink daily green smoothies) have been vegan for many years and don't suffer from deficiency either.

Like most things dealing with health, there is some conflicting information on whether plants contain any B12, or if it's created from bacteria in a healthy intestinal tract, or if it's only available via an omnivorous diet. The only way to know for sure is to get tested. Aside from that, maintain a complete diet of mostly fresh, whole foods and you'll most likely be just fine.

Should I always add a type of fat to my green smoothies? If so, which is best?

Green smoothies are perfectly fine with just greens, fruit, and water—especially if you're not used to consuming greens and your goal is simply to introduce them as a key player to your diet. However, I like to add some type of healthy fat to most of my smoothies, as it not only gives them a thicker, smoothie-like texture, but it also helps with the absorption of fat-soluble vitamins like K and E as well as minerals. The introduction of healthy fat also helps with satiation, too.

Some of the healthiest fats that can be included in green smoothies are avocado, virgin coconut oil, extra virgin olive oil, and occasionally nut butter made from soaked and peeled almonds.

If you subscribe to the food combining rules (or better yet, if you've tested them for yourself and found certain fats to cause excess gas and bloating with certain sugars) then fat is not supposed to be eaten with sugars. I recommend slowly incorporating fats to test for reactions. Generally, this is only an issue when combining starchy vegetables like sweet potato and squash with sweet fruits and some fat. At any rate, if you give your body some time to acclimate, I have found very few issues with food combining.

I just started drinking green and I have excess gas/green stools/headaches/bloating/etc. What am I doing wrong?

Probably nothing. The excess gas and bloating can come from a few different things. Try reducing the amount of fats you're using as well as fruit skins and see if that makes a difference. If so, try gradually adding them back. Also, be mindful of starchy greens like sweet potato and squash. The green stools could be because your stomach acid is so low that much is just passing through. This should correct itself over time, but you should look into taking probiotics and consult your doctor. The headaches are most likely due to one or more of the following: You're not used to so much fructose from the fruits, you're not consuming sufficient calories, and/or your body is ridding itself of all the built up toxins (detoxing) which can often make one feel worse than before the healthy transition. This too should dissipate with time.

Organic is expensive. Can't I just thoroughly wash my fruits and greens?

Absolutely. But keep in mind that organic is usually grown in soil with a higher mineral content so organic fruits and greens often contain a great deal more nutrition than non-organic. Also, organic doesn't always mean "pesticide-free." In fact, pesticides made from naturally occurring chemicals are just fine in the eyes of the law, even if the EPA deems them toxic in any way.

Can I survive and be healthy on green smoothies alone?

I don't know for certain and I probably never will. However, I do know that rotating your greens to avoid alkaloid toxicity is essential. But whether a person can live a healthy life on smoothies alone seems a recipe for tooth decay (from no use), and a jaw so weak that talking would become a chore. It may be possible (people have survived on much less), but I certainly wouldn't recommend it.

What about those pre-packaged smoothie mixes in the frozen section of local markets or smoothies from a juice bar or juice/smoothie chain store? Are those just as good?

The pre-packaged smoothie mixes in the frozen section of your local grocery store are absolutely awful. They don't contain any greens and most of them are full of added sugar, yogurt, corn starch, and other preservatives. Skip these.

Smoothie shops, however, do contain one or two options with greens in them but in my experience (in Los Angeles), the chain stores only offer greens in the form of powders. I made the mistake of trying one and had to return it. It was gritty and tasted like garbage. Until these places offer fresh, whole fruits and greens without added sugar and syrups, you'd be wise to pass.

GREEN SMOOTHIES AND PROTEIN DRINK RECIPES

The recipes in this book are great standalones and a wonderful jumping off point, but my hope is that you will use these as templates for your own concoctions and play with different pairings and additions. Below I have included some useful tips for preparing your green smoothies and protein drinks.

- Try adding fats to those that don't already have any listed. Some good options are extra virgin olive oil, avocado, coconut (oil, milk, and meat), and nut butters.

- Add superfoods to incorporate nutritious foods you otherwise would pass over like acai berries, aloe vera, cayenne, raw chocolate, bee pollen, flaxseed, garlic, ginger, pumpkin, and wheatgrass.

- Feel free to blend up apple seeds and other semi-soft fruit seeds if you have a high-powered blender. Never attempt to blend hard pits and seeds or large semi-soft pits like avocado.

- Leave the green tops on strawberries.

- Carrot tops are highly nutritious.

- Most blenders will work just fine, however, to blend waxier leaves (like kale), seeds, nuts, and other harder fruits, you will want to get a pro model blender. My favorites are Blendtec and Vitamix. (I have used both quite extensively and can't say I noticed a bit of difference between the two aside from appearance.) A stronger blender will also increase cellular wall breakdown of your fruits and greens thereby increasing nutrient availability.

- If your green smoothie comes out too foamy or looks like the contents are separating, it is likely because of the type of fiber in the smoothie. Insoluble fiber does that. So, try adding a bit of soluble fiber to bind it up. My go-to choices are banana, mango, and avocado. You can also eliminate the foam by setting the finished smoothie in the refrigerator for 10 minutes or so.

- The recipes in this book do not contain yields because that all depends on the amount of water/ice you use to achieve your desired consistency. The amount you drink in one sitting is up to you depending on your goals, size, and palate. Experimentation is your friend. Enjoy.

- Some recipes will contain added protein supplements in the ingredients list and some will suggest a good type of protein supplement to add if you choose to turn the green smoothie into a meal-replacement or post workout drink.

Blueberry Muffin

1 cup fresh/frozen blueberries

½ cup canned pumpkin

2 figs

1 banana

2-3 large kale leaves stemmed

1 tbsp chia seeds

1 cup coconut water

Blend until smooth. Adjust
liquid/ice as necessary.

 *Post Work-out*

Sweet Hot Margarita

2 cups watermelon

1 lemon (peeled or juiced)

1 large handful arugula

¼ jalapeño (or to taste)

dash of cayenne

1 tsp. agave nectar (or to taste)

2 cups ice

Blend until smooth. Add more water or ice if necessary. Pour into chili-powder-rimmed glass with ice cubes.

Avo-Cooler

1 bunch watercress

3-6 large mint leaves

1 lime (peeled or juiced)

1 cucumber

½ avocado

Blend until smooth. Add ice or water to thin.

 *Beauty*

Greens Lover

Peach Punch

2 peaches

1 mango

1 bunch lettuce (red leaf or mixed)

Remove the mango skin and all pits (stones). Blend with water or ice.

Optional Protein: Whey protein powder

 Kids/Beginner

Mangonut Kiwiberry

2–3 large kale leaves (stemmed)

3–5 strawberries

1 mango

1 cup young coconut meat

1 kiwi

Remove kiwi and mango skins and pit (stone). Blend and add coconut water/ice as necessary.

 Kids/Beginner

Honey Bunch

1-2 cups honeydew

¼ avocado

1 large handful spinach

1 medium cucumber

Blend with water and ice to
desired consistency.

 Beauty

Kids/Beginner

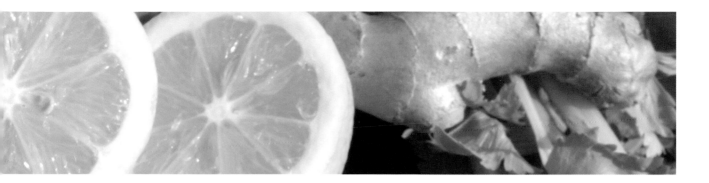

Salsa Fresca

1 cup cilantro

1 cup parsley

½ lemon (peeled)

1 apple

ginger to taste

1-2 stalks celery

Blend with water to desired consistency.

Fruit Cocktail

2 cups watermelon

1 cup strawberries

1 cup grapes

3-5 leaves of mint

1 large handful mixed greens

Blend with ice. Add more watermelon for desired consistency.

 Kids/Beginner

Plumkin

1-2 spoonfuls pumpkin purée

1-2 plums (pitted)

1 large handful spinach

cinnamon to taste

2 cups coconut water

Blend and add more coconut water as necessary.

Optional Protein: Whole milk plain yogurt

 *Beauty*

Add whole milk, chia seeds, or your favorite protein powder to make the perfect post-workout recovery green smoothie.

Col. Mustard Greens

2 cups mustard greens

2-3 roma tomatoes

¼ avocado

1 small zucchini

1 lime

favorite herbs to taste

Blend with water to desired consistency.

 *Savory*

Works well with fresh oregano, basil, or dill, but feel free to experiment with other fresh herbs.

What-A-Lemon

2-4 cups watermelon

1 bunch watercress

1 roma tomato

½ lemon

1 tbsp. olive oil

Blend with ice to desired
consistency.

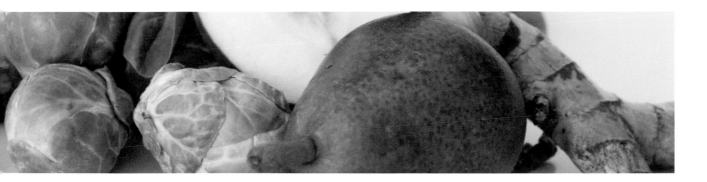

Apple Sprouts

¼ of a small red onion

1 apple

1 pear

1 handful spinach

3-4 brussels sprouts

ginger to taste

Blend with water and ice to desired consistency.

 *Greens Lover*

Sangria Blanca

1-2 white peaches (pitted)

1 cup rainier cherries (pitted)

1-2 white nectarines (pitted)

1 cup green grapes

6-10 endive leaves

3-5 mint leaves

Blend with water and ice to
desired consistency.

 *Kids/Beginner*

Mangomole

1 mango

1 peach

1 handful spinach

1 small bunch cilantro

¼ small onion

¼ avocado

½ yellow bell pepper

jalapeño to taste

½ lemon (peeled)

Blend with water and ice to desired consistency.

 *Greens Lover*

Gazpatcho

1-2 roma tomatoes
½ red bell pepper
1 garlic clove
¼ small onion
1 handful cilantro
1 handful parsley
jalapeño to taste
tarragon to taste

Blend with water and ice to
desired consistency.

 *Greens Lover*

Savory

Cosmo Chiller

1-2 cups mustard greens

1 medium cucumber

1 cup frozen cranberries

1 lime (peeled)

½ lemon (peeled)

3-5 mint leaves

Blend with water and ice to desired consistency.

 *Greens Lover*

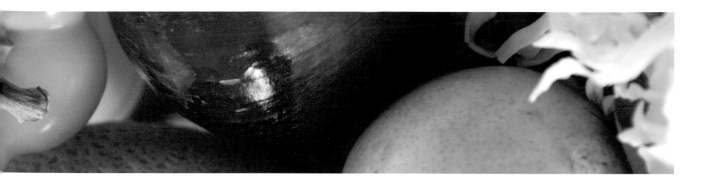

Golden Pear

1 pear

1-2 cups cantaloupe

½ yellow bell pepper

¼ small red onion

1 cup mustard greens

3-4 cabbage leaves

Blend with water and ice to
desired consistency.

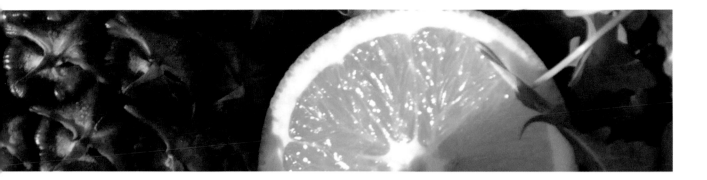

Tropicana

1 handful arugula

1 orange

½ yellow bell pepper

1-2 cups pineapple

1 handful spinach

Blend with water and ice to desired consistency.

Tup-Aloe Honey

1-2 cups honeydew melon

1-2 aloe leaves (peeled)

1 kiwi (peeled)

1 small bunch parsley

1 large handful mixed greens

Blend with water and ice to desired consistency.

 *Beauty*

Simply Sweet

2-4 kale leaves (de-stemmed)

1-2 cups strawberries

1 banana

Blend with water and ice to desired consistency.

Optional Protein: Whey protein powder

 Kids/Beginner

Sweet Mint

1-2 large collard leaves

1 pear

1 kiwi (pecled)

1 cup blackberries

1 cup blueberries

3-6 mint leaves

Blend with water and ice to
desired consistency.

Optional Protein: Chia seeds

 *Kids/Beginner*

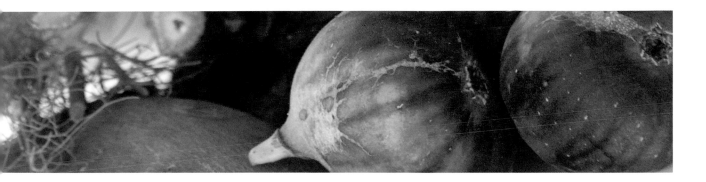

Figgy Cookie

1 bunch red leaf lettuce

½ cup fennel

1 cup sweet potato (pre-cooked)

2–3 figs

1 tbsp. almond butter

1–2 cups coconut water

nutmeg to taste

vanilla yogurt (optional)

Blend with ice to desired consistency.

Delectable Hulk

1 large handful spinach

2 kiwis

2-4 large basil leaves

1 banana

Blend with water and ice to
desired consistency.

 *Kids/Beginner*

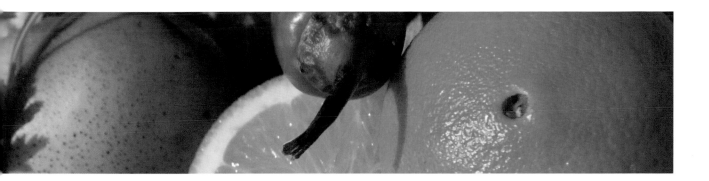

Mangorita

1 mango
1 orange (peeled)
1 large handful spinach
1 small handful parsley
1 small handful cilantro
jalapeño to taste

Blend with water and ice to
desired consistency.

 *Greens Lover*

Piña Kale-ada

1 cup pineapple

1 orange (peeled)

2 leaves rainbow chard

2 kale leaves (stemmed)

1 banana

1 cup coconut milk

Blend with ice to desired consistency.

Optional Protein: Whey protein powder

Beauty Booster

1 large handful spinach

1 small bunch turnip greens

2 tbsp. puréed pumpkin

2-4 dates (pitted)

1 tbsp. flax seed (or oil)

1 cup coconut milk

honey to taste (optional)

Blend with water and ice to desired consistency.

 *Beauty*

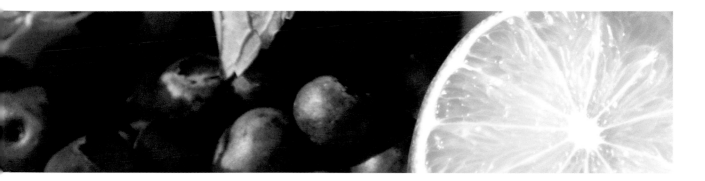

Rockin' Berry

1 handful arugula

1 cup grapes

1 cup blueberries

1 lime (peeled)

2-3 mint leaves

Blend with water and ice to desired consistency.

 Kids/Beginner

Old Fashioned

1 cup collards

½ grapefruit

1 orange

1 tbsp. honey

cayenne pepper to taste

Blend with ice to desired
consistency.

Georgia Peach

1 handful spinach

1 cup collards

1-2 peaches (pitted)

1 apple

ginger to taste

Blend with water and ice to desired consistency.

 Kids/Beginner

Chili Down

1 bunch dandelion greens

2-3 roma tomatoes

1 lemon (peeled)

1 tbsp. olive oil

chili powder to taste

Blend with water and ice to desired consistency.

 *Savory*

Greens Lover

Orange Jewelius

1 large handful mixed greens

1 orange

2-4 mint leaves

2-3 large basil leaves

½ lemon (peeled)

½ cup young coconut meat

Blend with water and ice to desired consistency.

 *Kids/Beginner*

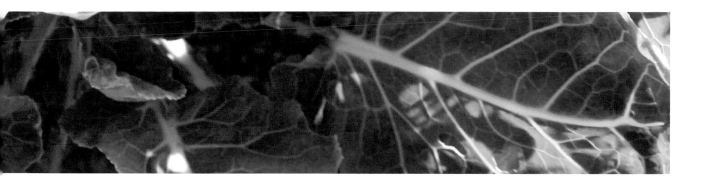

Man-Go-Green

1 mango
½ grapefruit (peeled)
1 kiwi (peeled)
1 cup chopped collards
3-5 large basil leaves

Blend with water and ice to
desired consistency.

 *Greens Lover*

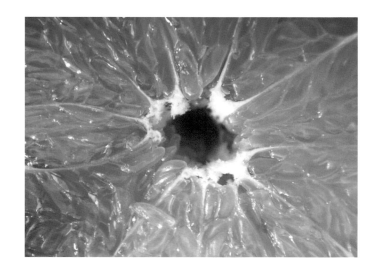

Superfood Fix

1 cup chopped kale

1 cup spinach

1 cup blueberry

2-3 tbsp. frozen acai

2-3 strawberries

1 cup cantaloupe

1 cup brewed green tea

1 tbsp. flax oil

Blend with water and ice to desired consistency.

 *Beauty*

Greens Lover

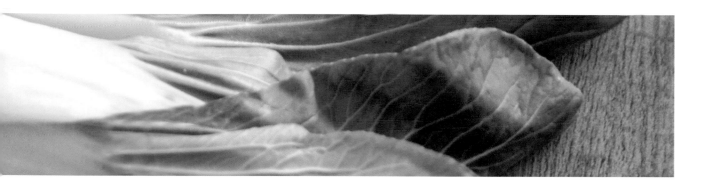

Ginger Drop

2 bok choy bulbs

thumb of peeled ginger

1 garlic clove

½-1 lemon (peeled)

honey to taste

Blend with water and ice to
desired consistency.

Feeling a little under the weather?
This drink is great for fighting an
oncoming cold.

Orange Crush

2 handfuls spinach

1 orange (peeled)

1 cup young coconut flesh

Blend with water and ice to desired consistency.

Optional Protein: Hemp protein powder

 *Kids/Beginner*

Wild Honey

3-4 large kale leaves (stemmed)

2-4 large basil leaves

1 cup blackberries

1 banana

1 tbsp. honey

Blend with water and ice to desired consistency.

Optional Protein: Whole milk plain yogurt

 *Kids/Beginner*

Chard Candy

2-4 chard leaves

1-2 cups red grapes

2-3 dates (pitted)

1 tbsp. almond butter

Blend with water and ice to desired consistency.

Optional Protein: Whole, raw milk

Cocoa Mo

2-3 kale leaves (stemmed)

1 handful mixed greens

1 apple

1 banana

1 tbsp. almond butter

1-2 tbsp. raw cocoa powder

vanilla to taste

Blend with water and ice to desired consistency.

Optional Protein: Egg protein powder

Vanilla extract is fine, but try to get find some vanilla beans and cut them open, scrape out the insides, and use that instead. They're delicious and you rid yourself of the alcohol used in extracts, however little there is.

Summer Citrus Crush

3-4 kale leaves

1 mango

1 orange

½ grapefruit

Peel the mango, orange, and grapefruit and toss the mango pit. Blend with water and ice to desired consistency.

 *Kids/Beginner*

Sweet Chard O' Mine

2-4 chard leaves

1-2 stalks celery

1 pear

1 cup raspberries

½ lemon (juice)

Blend with water and ice to desired consistency.

Banana Rock

1 handful arugula

2-3 kale leaves

½ cup pumpkin

1 pear

1 banana

Blend with water and ice to desired consistency.

Optional Protein: Hemp protein powder

Raspberry Pearée

1 bunch dandelion

½ cup fennel

1 pear

1 cup raspberries

1 banana

ginger to taste

Blend with water and ice to
desired consistency.

 *Greens Lover*

Coffee Greens

2 leaves kale

2 leaves chard

1 banana

1 cup macadamia nuts

1 cup brewed coffee

raw cocoa powder to taste

Blend with more brewed coffee
and ice to desired consistency.

**Optional Protein: Whole, raw
milk**

Good Apples

1 bunch dandelion greens

1 golden apple

1 banana

Blend with water and ice to desired consistency.

 *Greens Lover*

Pomapple

1 handful beet greens

2 apples

1 cup pomegranate seeds

Blend with water and ice to desired consistency.

 *Beauty*

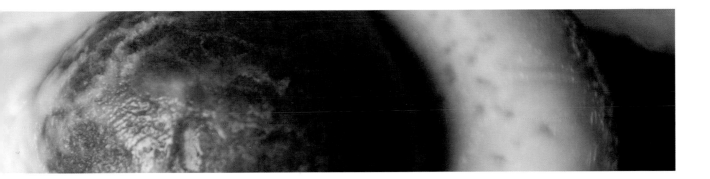

Proconut

2–4 kale leaves

¼ avocado

1 banana

1 cup coconut water

1 tbsp. chia seeds

1 scoop protein powder (optional)

Blend with water and ice to
desired consistency.

 *Post Work-out*

Santa Sangria

1 bunch wild oak
1 mango (pitted)
1 cup red grapes
1 orange (peeled)
1 plum (pitted)
1 lime (peeled)
1 cup pomegranate seeds

Blend with water and ice to
desired consistency.

 *Kids/Beginner*

Blind Date

1 cup chopped mustard greens

1 cup broccoli sprouts

½–1 lemon (peeled)

2–3 dates (pitted)

1 banana

Blend with water and ice to
desired consistency.

 *Greens Lover*

We Got The Beet

1 handful beet greens
1 cup red grapes
1 apple
1 banana

Blend with water and ice to desired consistency.

 *Kids/Beginner*

Shake It Up

1 cup turnip greens

1 cup broccoli sprouts

1 small zucchini

1 pear

1 cup young coconut meat

1 lime (peeled)

ginger to taste

Blend with water and ice to
desired consistency.

 *Greens Lover*

Resources

The Encyclopedia of Healing Foods by Michael T. Murray, N.D.
www.hgdbook.com/healing-foods

Blendtec Blender
www.hgdbook.com/blendtec

Vitamix Blender
www.hgdbook.com/vitamix

The 4-Hour Body by Timothy Ferriss
www.hgdbook.com/4-hour-body

Primal Blueprint 101
http://www.marksdailyapple.com/primal-blueprint-101/

The Coconut Oil Miracle by Bruce Fife, N.D.
www.hgdbook.com/coconut-miracle

User's Guide to Protein and Amino Acids (Basic Health Publications) by Keri Marshall, N.D.
www.hgdbook.com/amino-acids

Local Food Systems: Concepts, Impacts, and Issues
http://www.ers.usda.gov/publications/err-economic-research-report/err97.aspx

The Protein Power Lifeplan by Michael R. & Mary Dan Eades, M.D.
www.hgdbook.com/protein-power

Find Food Coops
http://www.localharvest.org/food-coops/

The World's Healthiest Foods List
www.whfoods.com

USDA National Nutrient Database for Standard Reference
www.hgdbook.com/nutrient-data
www.nal.usda.gov/fnic/foodcomp/search/